SHRED IT!

FREE FALL

EXTREME SKYDIVING

Virginia Loh-Hagan

45TH PARALLEL PRESS

Ann Arbor, Michigan

www.cherrylakepublishing.com

Content Adviser: Liv Williams, Editor, iLivExtreme

Reading Adviser: Beth Walker Gambro, MS, Ed., Reading Consultant, Yorkville, IL

Photo Credits: © Sky Antonio/Shutterstock, cover, title page; © US Army Photo/Alamy, 5; © Vladimir Zhoga/Shutterstock, 6; © Mauricio Graiki/Shutterstock, 7; © Sky Antonio/Shutterstock, 9; © Everett Collection/Shutterstock, 11; Unknown author, Public domain, via Wikimedia Commons, 12; U.S. Air Force, 15; © Pictorial Press Ltd/Alamy, 16; © sirtravelalot/Shutterstock, 17; © ViktorKozlov/Shutterstock, 18–19; © Sky Antonio/Shutterstock, 20; © Seliverstov Andrey/Shutterstock, 21; © from the book *Escape or Die* by Anthony Martin, 22; © Mauricio Graiki/Shutterstock, 25; © Ewan Cowie Photography, 26–27; © ZUMA Press, Inc./Alamy, 28; © 615 collection/Alamy, 29

Library of Congress Cataloging-in-Publication Data has been filed and is available at catalog.loc.gov

Cherry Lake Press would like to acknowledge the work of the Partnership for 21st Century Learning, a Network of Battelle for Kids. Please visit Battelle for Kids online for more information.

Printed in the United States of America

Note from publisher: Websites change regularly, and their future contents are outside of our control. Supervise children when conducting any recommended online searches for extended learning opportunities.

ABOUT THE AUTHOR

Virginia Loh-Hagan is an author, university professor, former classroom teacher, and curriculum designer. In college, she jumped off a bunk bed and broke her toe. No more jumping for her. She lives in San Diego with her very tall husband and very naughty dogs.

Table of Contents

CHAPTER 1

Humans Can Fly!

It's a bird! It's a plane! It's a…skydiver? It was December 2010. People looked up at the night sky. They saw strange, bright lights. Many reported an **unidentified** flying object, or **UFO**. Unidentified means unknown.

People thought they saw an alien ship. But Jon Devore and Sean MacCormac are not aliens. They are skydivers. They skydived at night. They used **flares**. Flares are devices that produce bright lights. That's what people saw!

Skydiving teams perform with flares or sparklers to light up the night.

Skydivers jump from planes. They jump from 16,000 feet (4,877 meters) or higher above the ground. They **free fall** at first. A free fall is when nothing slows a fall. But skydiving doesn't feel like falling. It feels like floating or flying.

Skydivers open a **parachute**. A parachute is a large device made of strong, thin cloth. It slows a fall through the air. Skydivers steer the parachute. They land in areas called **drop zones**. These are designated places to land.

SHRED IT! ADVICE FROM THE FIELD:

Use Signals

Skydivers have to respect each other. They avoid being on top of other skydivers. They don't want to fall into someone else's parachute. They give a wave-off signal. They make sure everyone is away from them. Then they hold out their pointer finger to signal that it's time to deploy a parachute. Skydivers have other hand signals. Some skydivers get nervous when they're free falling. So other skydivers hold their hand in a fist, and then extend their pinkie finger and thumb. This can mean "relax." Skydiving instructors sometimes pat the tops of their students' heads. This means "stay calm."

AN INSTRUCTOR AND STUDENT ON A JUMP

Skydivers must carry 2 parachutes. One is the main parachute. If there is a problem, they use the other parachute. It is a backup.

Some skydivers wear **wingsuits**. These are one-piece outfits with webbing under the arms and between the legs. Wingsuits help skydivers fall more slowly than they normally would in a free fall. This means they get to fly longer. They still need a parachute, though.

Jay Stokes loves skydiving. He was an Army Green Beret. They are trained to skydive. Stokes trained others. He trained instructors. He has completed over 27,000 jumps. He set world records. He was part of the largest night dive. He also made the most jumps ever in 24 hours. He made 640 jumps! He jumped about every 2 minutes. He used 3 airplanes. They took him back into the sky. Later, he tried to break his record. The weather stopped him.

The highest skydive was from 135,898 feet (41,422 m)!

Some extreme skydivers jump from higher **altitudes**, or heights. These skydivers jump from 30,000 feet (9,144 m) or higher. Air is thinner at that height. Divers need oxygen masks and tanks.

But it's worth it. That's what extreme skydiving is all about. The longer the free fall, the better.

CHAPTER 2

A History of Skydiving Daredevils

Flying machines were invented long ago. **Daredevils** wanted to fly, too. Daredevils are people who take risks.

People started riding in hot air balloons. Daredevils jumped out of them. In 1797, André-Jacques Garnerin jumped from a balloon. He was strapped to a big parachute. He did stunts in the air.

Airplanes first flew in 1903. Daredevils were jumping out of them in no time. Leslie Irvin did the first free fall in 1919. He did stunts for movies. He proved that skydivers could be in control when the parachute opened.

Huge crowds gathered to see early daredevils in action.

Early skydivers performed in shows. They jumped from planes. They walked on the airplane's wings. This was called barnstorming. It was like a flying circus. The military also helped develop skydiving. Skydiving saved the lives of airplane crews. It also delivered soldiers to the battlefield.

Georgia "Tiny" Broadwick was a popular barnstormer. She was the first woman to jump from a plane. She was also the first woman to do a free fall. She broke bones. She hurt her shoulder. She landed in swamps. She was dragged by her parachute. She jumped from a burning balloon. She said, "I was never afraid. I'd go up any time, any place. The only thing I hated was getting back to earth so quickly."

EXTREME SKYDIVING:

Know the Lingo

Arch: a skydiving position

Canopy: the umbrella part of the parachute

Climbout: being mostly outside the plane door and getting ready to jump

Cork: losing control and falling quickly

Dock: making contact with another skydiver in free fall

Drogue: a smaller parachute to slow down falling

Hook turn: a steep dive

Jump run: the flight of the airplane

Opening point: the moment when a skydiver opens the parachute

Pack: preparing a parachute system before jumping

Relative work: when two or more people meet in midair

Rig: the parachute system

Ripcord: a metal cable that opens the parachute

Water jump: landing in water

Whuffo: someone who is not a skydiver

CHAPTER 3

There's a Style for Every Skydiver!

There are many ways to skydive. Skydivers choose the style they find the most thrilling. They choose what challenges them.

HALO

HIGH ALTITUDE LOW OPENING JUMP

HALO means High Altitude Low Opening jump. Skydivers free fall for several minutes. They open their parachutes very close to the ground. The U.S. military developed HALO. They didn't want soldiers to be seen by enemies.

HAHO

HIGH ALTITUDE HIGH OPENING JUMP

HAHO is another skydiving jump developed by the military. HAHO means High Altitude High Opening jump. Skydivers open their parachutes soon after jumping. They glide for long distances before landing.

Another way to take skydiving to the extreme is through **formation** skydiving. A formation is a planned arrangement. Formation skydiving is also called belly-flying. Skydivers' bellies face toward Earth. Skydivers create shapes and patterns in free fall. They join in the air. Skydivers hold each other's arms or legs. There can be 2 or more skydivers. Sometimes they do tricks.

FORMATION SKYDIVING

FREE-FLYING

Free-flying is when a skydiver flies in any way that's not belly-flying. Skydivers do tricks in the air. They stand up. They fly upside down. They fly over each other. They fly under each other. They fly around each other. They also make formations.

FREESTYLE SKYDIVING

Freestyle skydiving is like ballet. Skydivers dance in free fall. They do loops and spins. Freestyle skydivers work in 2-person teams. One diver does the tricks and the other films them. A camera is attached to their helmet.

Another type of skydiving is **swooping**. Skydivers swoop through the air. "Swoopers" jump from lower in the sky. They jump from 5,000 feet (1,524 m). They open their high-speed canopy quickly. They fly fast and low before landing. Flying low makes it dangerous.

SWOOPING

SHRED IT!

When Extreme Is Too Extreme!

Anthony Martin handcuffed his hands to a belt around his waist on August 6, 2013. His right arm was chained to the inside of a coffin. He locked himself in the coffin. He used a prison door lock. There was no key. Two skydivers held the handles of the coffin and jumped out of a plane. They were 14,500 feet (4,420 m) above ground. They were in free fall. The coffin moved a lot. Martin picked the lock. He struggled to open the door. He escaped! He somersaulted out of the coffin. He opened his parachute. He landed safely. Martin is an escape artist. He was inspired by famous magician Harry Houdini. This was the second time Martin had tried this trick. He had only skydived 17 times before this trick. He works on not being scared. He said, "Fear is one of those emotions that kind of distracts from your ability to think clearly and be effective."

ANTHONY MARTIN

CHAPTER 4

Keep Shredding!

Skydiving is thrilling. It's also dangerous.

Skydivers get hurt for different reasons. Some skydivers do unsafe things. They do stunts before they're ready. Some make mistakes. They don't steer correctly. They don't pack their gear correctly.

Instructors keep students safe while they go through training.

Changing winds affect landing speed. This means skydivers can lose control of their parachutes. Sometimes, parachutes hit each other. Skydiving from high places is dangerous. Planes can crash. Skydivers can also get sick from being so high. They lose oxygen.

But skydivers are still taking leap after leap!

Skydiving teams are always working on breaking records. They try to dive in new ways. They try to dive in larger groups. In 2024, a team at Skydive Arizona set a head-up world record. The team was called "Stand Together." They had 96 skydivers as part of their formation. The previous record was 84.

In 2012, Felix Baumgartner was the first skydiver to break the sound barrier. He died tragically in 2025 while paragliding.

Some skydivers are looking for something more extreme. Some are making **stratosphere** jumps. The stratosphere is the second-lowest layer of Earth's atmosphere. Some are jumping without parachutes. Luke Aikins did this in 2016. He jumped into a huge net. Marco Hepp set a speed skydiving record in 2022. He went 329.2 miles (429.8 kilometers) per hour!

What's the next extreme? Skydiving from space? There are no limits for skydivers.

SHRED IT! SPOTLIGHT:

Cheryl Stearns

Cheryl Stearns was born in 1955. She's been skydiving since age 17. And she's still going! That's a long time to love free falling. She has accomplished many goals in her skydiving career. She was the first female member of the U.S. Army Golden Knights. This is an elite parachute team. Stearns holds the Guinness World Record for woman with the most parachute jumps in 24 hours. She made 352 jumps between November 8 and 9 in 1995. She also holds a world record for most total skydiving jumps made by a woman. She has made over 22,000 jumps! On top of these records, she was the U.S. Parachuting champion 37 times. She was inducted into the Skydiving Hall of Fame in 2010. And she's not just a skydiver. She's also an accomplished pilot and flight instructor.

CHERYL STEARNS

DID YOU KNOW?

- The military trains dogs to skydive. They jump with an officer. Dogs are trained to smell hidden bombs. They are also trained to find victims of plane crashes. Dogs travel with cameras to send pictures back to the military.

- Leonardo da Vinci was the first person to think of a parachute. He drew a picture of a parachute in 1495. He dreamed of humans being able to fly. He designed gliders.

- Flying squirrels have flaps of skin like a wingsuit. This is how they fly from tree to tree. Skydivers wearing wingsuits look like flying squirrels.

- Former President George H. W. Bush skydived for his 85th and 90th birthdays.

- People have done some strange things while skydiving. One person got a tattoo while in a free fall. Another got a haircut.

CONSIDER THIS!

TAKE A POSITION! Many professional athletes have contracts. They are not allowed to do extreme sports like skydiving. Their teams are afraid they'll get hurt. These athletes can't put their bodies at risk. They need to be able to play their sports. If they skydive, they could get in trouble. Do you think this is fair? What do you think about this issue? Argue your point with reasons and evidence.

SAY WHAT? Learn more about BASE jumping. BASE jumping also involves jumping from high places. How are BASE jumping and skydiving similar? How are they different?

THINK ABOUT IT! "Full contact skydiving" combines skydiving and martial arts. It's like fighting in the air. Some people thought this was a real sport. But it was a joke. No one actually does it. Create a new skydiving sport. What would you call it? What would be some of the moves?

SEE A DIFFERENT SIDE! Skydivers jump because they like the feeling of being free. They like the excitement of doing something dangerous. Learn more about the dangers of skydiving. Do you think the dangers are greater than the rewards?

LEARN MORE

BOOKS

Kelliher, Lauren. *Would You Rather...Go Skydiving or Cliff Diving?.. and Other Daring Questions About Exploits, Feats, and Stunts.* Chicago, IL: World Book, Inc., 2023.

Vonder Brink, Tracy. *Skydiving.* Minneapolis, MN: Jump!, Inc., 2025.

WEBSITES

With an adult, explore more online with these suggested searches.

National Skydiving League

Red Bull | Skydiving: Are these the 8 most incredible clips of all time?

GLOSSARY

altitudes (AL-tuh-toodz) the height of something above sea level

daredevils (DAIR-deh-vuhlz) risk-takers

drop zones (DRAHP ZOHNZ) designated places to land

flares (FLAIRZ) devices that produce bright lights

formation (for-MAY-shuhn) an arrangement of a group of people

free fall (FREE-fahl) to fly in the air after jumping and before landing

parachute (PAR-uh-shoot) a piece of strong, light fabric attached to thin ropes that helps skydivers slow their fall through the air

sound barrier (SOWND BAIR-ee-er) the force of air that pushes back harder as something gets close to the speed of sound

stratosphere (STRAH-tuh-sfeer) the second-lowest layer of Earth's atmosphere

swooping (SWOOP-ing) sweeping through the air

UFO (YOO-EFF-OH) unidentified flying object

unidentified (uhn-ahy-DEN-tuh-fied) unknown

wingsuits (WING-soots) one-piece flight outfits with webbing under the arms and between the legs

INDEX